✳ Smithsonian

READERS

World of Wonder

LEVEL 3

The Planets

Ancient Egypt

Rain Forest Animals

Wild Weather

The United States

Sharks

Silver Dolphin Books
An imprint of Printers Row Publishing Group
10350 Barnes Canyon Road, Suite 100, San Diego, CA 92121
www.silverdolphinbooks.com

Printers Row Publishing Group is a division of Readerlink Distribution Services, LLC.
Silver Dolphin Books is a registered trademark of Readerlink Distribution Services, LLC.

All notations of errors or omissions should be addressed to Silver Dolphin Books, Editorial Department, at the above address.

ISBN: 978-1-62686-453-5
Manufactured, printed, and assembled in Dongguan City, China
20 19 18 17 16   3 4 5 6 7

Sharks! written by Brenda Scott Royce
Wild Weather and *Rain Forest Animals* written by Emily Rose Oachs
The United States and *Ancient Egypt* written by Courtney Acampora
The Planets written by Ruth Strother
Edited by Kaitlyn DiPerna
Editorial Assistance by Courtney Acampora
Cover Design by Jenna Riggs
Cover Production by Rusty von Dyl
Book Design by Marc Jacobs
Sharks!, *Wild Weather,* and *Rain Forest Animals* reviewed by Dr. Don E. Wilson,
        Curator Emeritus of the Department of Vertebrate Zoology, National
        Museum of Natural History, Smithsonian
The United States and *Egypt* reviewed by F. Robert van der Linden, chairman of the
        Aeronautics Division, National Air and Space Museum, Smithsonian
The Planets reviewed by Andrew K. Johnston, Geographer for the Center for Earth
        and Planetary Studies, National Air and Space Museum, Smithsonian

For Smithsonian Enterprises:
Kealy Gordon, Product Development Manager, Licensing
Ellen Nanney, Licensing Manager
Brigid Ferraro, Vice President, Education and Consumer Products
Carol LeBlanc, Senior Vice President, Education and Consumer Products
Chris Liedel, President

HOW TO USE THIS BOOK

Glossary

As you read each title, you will see words in **bold letters**. More information about these words can be found in the glossary at the end of each title.

Quizzes

Multiple-choice quizzes are included at the end of each title. Use these quizzes to check your understanding of the topic. Answers are printed at the end of the quiz, or you can reread the title to check your answers.

Fact Cards

Each title comes with six tear-out fact cards. Read the cards for fun or use them as quizzes with a friend or family member. You'll be impressed with all you can learn!

ABOUT THE SMITHSONIAN

Founded in 1846, the Smithsonian is the world's largest museum and research complex, consisting of 19 museums and galleries, the National Zoological Park, and nine research facilities. The Smithsonian's vision is to shape the future by preserving our heritage, discovering new knowledge, and sharing our resources with the world.

SMITHSONIAN READER SERIES

Pre–Level 1
Read with Me!

Adorable Baby Animals

Under the Sea

Planes, Trains, and Trucks

What's the Weather Outside?

Life on a Farm

Bodies

Level 1
Early Adventures

Animal Habitats

Outer Space

Reptiles

Vehicles

Safari Animals

Insects

Level 2
Seriously Amazing

Nighttime Animals

Solar System

Baby Animals

Human Body

Dinosaurs and Other Prehistoric Creatures

Sea Life

Level 3
World of Wonder

Sharks!

Wild Weather

Rain Forest Animals

The United States

The Planets

Ancient Egypt

Level 4
Endless Explorations

The Science and History of Flight

Space Exploration

Natural Disasters

World Wonders

Ocean Habitats

Predators

CONTENTS

SHARKS

Sharks are among the world's most fascinating creatures.

Sharks are a type of fish. Like other fish, sharks swim by moving their bodies from side to side. Sharks need to swim in order to live. They get the oxygen they need from the water around them.

? DID YOU KNOW?

More than four hundred species of sharks live in the ocean. Each shark species has special features that make it unique.

At Home in the Ocean

Sharks are found in all of the world's oceans. They live in the deep dark ocean and in shallow coastal waters.

The Earth's oceans are all connected, and many sharks **migrate**, or travel long distances, in search of food or mates. Seasonal changes in water temperature are one reason sharks migrate. Blacktip sharks move south along the east coast of the United States every winter, seeking warmer waters.

Most sharks
prefer warm waters,
but Greenland sharks make
their home near the North Pole!
These huge, slow-moving sharks inhabit the icy
waters of the Arctic and North Atlantic Oceans.

Bull sharks are one of
the few shark species
that can survive in
fresh water for long
periods of time.
Bull sharks have been
known to travel long
distances up rivers,
including the Amazon,
the Mississippi, and
the Ganges.

Built to Swim

Sharks are ideally suited to a life at sea. Most have torpedo-shaped bodies that help them easily glide through water. A shark's powerful tail propels it forward. Its fins are used for steering and keeping the shark steady.

Sharks don't have bones; their skeletons are made of **cartilage**. Cartilage is lighter and more flexible than bone.

Shark's skeletons are made of the same material as human noses and ears.

? DID YOU KNOW?

Sharks get the oxygen they need from the water around them. Depending on the species, a shark has five to seven pairs of **gills**. These slit-like openings pull oxygen from the water. Most sharks breathe by swimming with their mouths open, which allows water to pass through their gills.

great white shark's gills

Shark skin appears smooth, but if you rub it the wrong way it feels like sandpaper. That's because shark skin is covered with tiny structures called **dermal denticles**. Dermal denticles are covered with enamel, just like human teeth, making shark skin very tough.
By channeling water, dermal denticles also increase a shark's swimming speed!

Tons of Teeth

Sharks produce new teeth throughout their entire lives. If a shark loses a tooth, they will replace it. In fact, they have rows of teeth waiting in line.

Some sharks lose up to thirty thousand teeth in their lifetime. A great white shark has three thousand teeth in its mouth at all times.

DID YOU KNOW?

Venice, Florida, is known as the "shark's tooth capital of the world" due to the large number of shark teeth that wash up on its sandy beaches every year.

Sharks are often feared because of their many sharp teeth. But not all sharks have large, razor-like teeth.

Whale sharks have rows of tiny teeth. They use their teeth like a rake to sift food from the water.

The flattened back teeth of horn sharks are great for crushing the shells of clams, crabs, snails, and other prey.

All Shapes and Sizes

Sharks come in many shapes and sizes.

The grey reef shark has the familiar torpedo shape that most people associate with sharks.

The angel shark is wide and flat.

A thresher shark's enormous curved tail takes up one-third of its body weight.

The whale shark is bigger than a schoolbus.

The pygmy dogshark is smaller than a shoebox.

How do these sharks stack up?

whale shark: 40 feet

great white: 20 feet

hammerhead: 13 feet

tiger shark: 10 feet

zebra shark: 9 feet

shortfin mako: 7 feet

frilled shark: 6 feet

tasseled wobbegong: 5½ feet

leopard shark: 4 feet

horn shark: 3 feet

cookie-cutter shark: 20 inches

pygmy dogshark: 7 inches

DID YOU KNOW?

In most shark species, females are larger than males.

Killer Fish

The great white shark is one of the most feared and aggressive sharks on the planet. It is an **apex predator**, the top of its **food chain**; no other animals eat it.

? DID YOU KNOW? Great white sharks have incredible senses that help them locate prey. They can detect blood from three miles away!

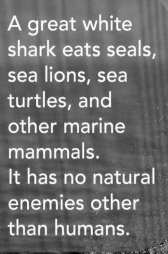

A great white shark eats seals, sea lions, sea turtles, and other marine mammals. It has no natural enemies other than humans.

Great white sharks are found in oceans around the world. They go on long migrations to look for food.

One great white shark traveled from South Africa to Australia and back—a distance of more than thirteen thousand miles—in about nine months. Scientists named this long-distance swimmer "Nicole" after actress Nicole Kidman, a shark fan.

Indian
Ocean

South
Africa

Australia

Gentle Giant

The whale shark is the biggest fish in the world. It can weigh more than forty thousand pounds.

Despite their name, whale sharks are gentle giants rather than fierce predators. They feed mainly on plankton and small fish. Plankton are tiny organisms that drift in the ocean. The whale shark swims along with its massive mouth open and just sucks them in.

? DID YOU KNOW?

A whale shark's mouth can be five feet wide— almost large enough for a small car to drive through!

Whale sharks have polka-dotted backs. Just as no two human fingerprints are the same, each whale shark has a unique pattern of spots. Scientists use special software to help identify an individual whale shark by its markings. This software was first developed by NASA to map the stars!

Whale sharks spend most of their time alone. But they sometimes gather in huge groups of hundreds of whale sharks to feed. Thanks to the whale shark's peaceful personality, scientists can observe these animals up close without danger.

Looks Like...

It's easy to see how these sharks got their names.

Hammerhead

This shark's unusual head, shaped somewhat like a hammer, is used to trap stingrays by pinning them down. Stingrays are the hammerhead's favorite food.

The hammerhead's eyes are at the ends of its head, allowing it to see all around, even above and below. It cannot, however, see straight ahead!

Bonnethead

The bonnethead, a member of the hammerhead family, has a rounded head. Its head is shaped like a woman's bonnet or a shovel blade (which is why bonnetheads are sometimes called shovelhead sharks).

Sawshark

This shark's snout looks like the blade of a chainsaw.
The sawshark uses its saw to dig prey out of sandy sea bottoms.
It will also move its head rapidly from side to side to slash at prey.

Sawsharks and sawfish look a lot alike—but only one of these animals is a shark. Sawfish are members of the ray family, along with stingrays and manta rays. The sawshark's barbels—a pair of whisker-like protrusions on the snout—are one way to tell them apart.

sawfish

Spots and Stripes

Tiger Shark)))))

The vertical stripes on young tiger sharks give this species its name. When the shark grows up, its stripes will fade or disappear. These aggressive sharks have sharp, curved teeth, which allow them to rip through the shells of sea turtles. They also eat other sharks, sea birds, and sea mammals.

Zebra Shark)))))

The zebra shark has stripes like a zebra when it is born. Like the tiger shark, the zebra shark loses its stripes when it reaches adulthood. Adult zebra sharks have spots instead of stripes.

baby zebra shark

Leopard Shark

Like a leopard found in a forest, the leopard shark is covered in spots. Because their mouths are located on the undersides of their heads, they can eat crabs, clams, and fish eggs as they swim along the ocean floor. The leopard shark's spots serve as camouflage, helping it blend in with its surroundings.

adult zebra shark

27

Weird and Wonderful

One of the strangest shark species on the planet, the cookie-cutter shark gets its name from its odd style of eating. It bites with its pointy lower teeth then spins its body around, slicing a circular chunk of flesh off a prey animal.

? DID YOU KNOW?

These small sharks have been known to attack animals much larger than themselves—including great white sharks!

With fringes that resemble seaweed, the tasseled wobbegong is a master of disguise. This odd-looking bottom-dweller blends right in with coral reefs and algae-covered rocks. When a fish swims within reach, the wobbegong opens its large mouth and sucks it in.

The bramble shark has thorny scales covering its body.

Can a shark glow in the dark? Tiny organs called photophores on the lanternshark's skin produce light.

The epaulette shark can swim, but it mainly moves by "walking" on the ocean bottom, using its fins as legs!

Shark Records

BIGGEST:

At more than forty feet long, the whale shark easily wins the prize for the biggest fish in the sea.

At about six inches in length, the dwarf lanternshark is most likely the world's smallest shark.

fastest:

The shortfin mako holds the record for fastest swimming speed by a shark. One mako was clocked at more than forty miles per hour.

strongest bite:

Bull sharks have the greatest bite strength of any shark, even beating out the great white!

deadliest diet:

Hammerhead sharks may have the most dangerous eating habits of any shark. Stingrays, their favorite food, have sharp venomous spines on their tails. One hammerhead was found with nearly a hundred stingray spines in its mouth!

deepest diver:

The Portuguese dogfish has been found at depths of nearly ten thousand feet.

Shark Ancestors

Sharks have been around for approximately four hundred million years. That's two hundred million years before dinosaurs roamed the earth!

While some types of shark have survived millions of years, others have gone **extinct**.

Megalodon illustration

The largest shark that ever lived was the Megalodon. This prehistoric predator may have reached sixty feet in length.

fossilized Megalodon shark tooth and great white shark tooth

Scientists can tell a lot about the Megalodon from **fossil** evidence. Fossilized Megalodon teeth measuring up to seven inches high have been found.

male falcatus fossil

Falcatus was a foot-long shark that lived over three hundred million years ago. Males had a forward-facing spine protruding from their backs. Females did not have this spine. Numerous falcatus fossils have been found in Montana, which was once beneath the sea.

? DID YOU KNOW? The oldest complete shark fossil found to date is over four hundred million years old. The ancient specimen of the *Doliodus problematicus,* a small shark measuring less than a foot in length, was found in New Brunswick, Canada.

shark fossil

Studying Sharks

Biologists have been using ROVs (remotely operated vehicles) for decades to get a better look at undersea life. ROVs can travel into waters that are too deep or dangerous for a human diver. In 2012, biologists using an ROV discovered a previously unknown shark species, the Galapagos catshark.

Despite using the latest technology to study sharks, there is still a lot to learn about these fascinating fish.

GPS (Global Positioning System) technology uses satellites to pinpoint locations anywhere on earth. Many cars are equipped with GPS devices, which help direct drivers to their destinations. Biologists are now using GPS on sharks!

A device containing a tiny transmitter is attached to the shark, allowing the shark's movements to be tracked. The data collected by these and other types of satellite tags help biologists learn more about shark behavior and migration patterns.

? DID YOU KNOW? You can go online to track the travel routes of tagged sharks. Some sharks even have their own Twitter accounts!

Threats to Sharks

Sharks play an important role in keeping our oceans healthy. When the top animal in a food chain disappears, its absence causes problems down the chain. If great white sharks were removed from an area, the number of seals (a favorite food item) would greatly increase. Too many hungry seals means not enough fish to go around. Eventually, the entire **ecosystem** would collapse.

What is the greatest threat to sharks? Humans. It is estimated that around one hundred million sharks are killed by humans each year.

Overfishing is the major cause of shark deaths each year. Because sharks grow slowly and only produce several young during their lifetime, more sharks are killed before they can grow their numbers.

One major cause of shark deaths is shark fin soup. Shark fin soup is a delicacy in parts of Asia. Fishermen catch sharks, cut off their fins, and throw their bodies back in the ocean. This is called finning.

To protect sharks from the practice of finning, the U.S. Congress passed the Shark Conservation Act in 2010. Several countries have banned shark fishing altogether.

Sharks! Quiz

1. Sharks are what type of animal?

   (a) Mammal
   (b) Fish
   (c) Whale
   (d) Amphibian

2. What shark can survive fresh water for long periods of time?

   (a) Tiger shark
   (b) Great white shark
   (c) Bull shark
   (d) Thresher shark

3. What causes shark skin to feel like sandpaper?

   (a) Dermal denticles
   (b) Barnacles
   (c) Algae
   (d) Hair

4. About how many teeth does a great white shark have in its mouth at all times?

   (a) 3,000
   (b) 150
   (c) 88
   (d) 1,237

5. Which is the largest shark?

   (a) Pygmy dogshark
   (b) Tiger Shark
   (c) Whale shark
   (d) Thresher shark

6. Which shark has an unusual head used to pin down prey?

   (a) Zebra shark
   (b) Hammerhead shark
   (c) Leopard shark
   (d) Bramble shark

7. What are photophores?

   (a) Tiny organisms that drift in the ocean
   (b) Spots on leopard sharks
   (c) Tiny organs that produce light
   (d) Remotely operated vehicles

8. What is the greatest threat to sharks?

   (a) Whales
   (b) Stingrays
   (c) Sea lions
   (d) Humans

Glossary

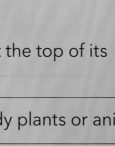

apex predator an animal at the top of its food chain; no animals eat it

biologists people who study plants or animals

cartilage light, flexible material from which a shark's skeleton is made

dermal denticles tiny tooth-like structures covering a shark's skin

ecosystem a community of all the living things in an area

extinct a species that no longer exists

food chain the order that animals eat plants and other animals

fossil a trace or print or the remains of a plant or animal preserved in earth or rock

gills organs used by fish that allow them to breathe underwater

migrate to move across long distances

GREAT WHITE SHARK

WHALE SHARK

HAMMERHEAD

LEOPARD SHARK

SHORTFIN MAKO

THRESHER SHARK

Favorite Foods: plankton, small fish, squid
Length: up to 40 feet
Weight: up to 44,000 pounds

Favorite Foods: seals, sea lions, dolphins
Length: up to 26 feet
Weight: up to 5,000 pounds

Favorite Foods: crabs, clams, fish eggs
Length: up to 6 feet
Weight: up to 50 pounds

Favorite Foods: stingrays, squid, fish, small sharks
Length: up to 20 feet
Weight: up to 1,000 pounds

Favorite Foods: herring, tuna, mackerel
Length: up to 24 feet
Weight: up to 750 pounds

Favorite Foods: mackerel, tuna, squid
Length: up to 13 feet
Weight: 1,200 pounds

Wild Weather

Emily Rose Oachs

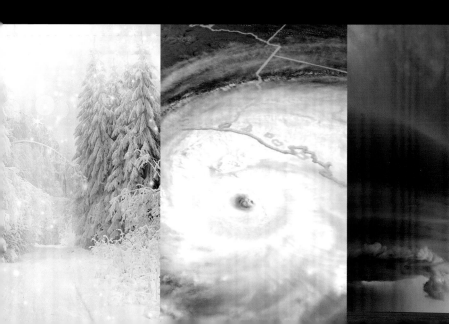

Contents

What Is Weather?

Weather is always all around you. Weather is the changing conditions of Earth's **atmosphere**.

hurricane

Some days are dark and stormy. Other days are bright and sunny. Every day has weather, and every day the weather changes.

sunny day

tornado

Weather affects you each day. It helps you decide what clothes to wear or what activities to do.

Tornadoes, hurricanes, and rain are just some examples of weather.

What Causes Weather?

Weather happens because of the sun. The sun heats the Earth's surface unevenly. Areas near the equator get a lot of heat from the sun.

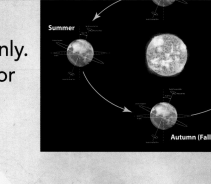

Seasons – Movement of the Earth and Sun

Spring

Summer

Winter

Autumn (Fall)

But little sunlight reaches the poles. So the poles get much less heat from the sun.

This uneven heating leads to all weather.

It leads to wind, clouds, temperature, humidity, precipitation, and air pressure. These six things combine to create many different types of weather.

Wind is the movement of air across the Earth.

Clouds are white and gray forms that hang in the sky.

Humidity is the **moisture** in the air.

Temperature is the amount of heat in an area.

Precipitation is water that falls from clouds as rain, snow, or hail.

Air pressure is the weight of the air at the Earth's surface.

Cumulus, Stratus, and Cirrus: Clouds

Clouds are made up of millions of tiny water droplets. Heat from the sun causes water from lakes, rivers, and oceans to **evaporate**. This water changes into a gas, entering the air. This evaporated water is called water vapor.

The water vapor rises into the atmosphere. It cools as it rises. Then the vapor **condenses** into tiny water droplets, forming clouds.

Cirrus clouds are thin, feathery clouds high in the atmosphere. Cirrus clouds usually come with nice weather.

Stratus clouds are gray clouds. They spread across the whole sky, like a blanket. Sometimes they produce a light rain called drizzle.

On some clear days, fluffy mounds of cumulus clouds dot the sky.

Some cumulus clouds, called *cumulonimbus* clouds, tower high into the sky. These tall, dark clouds usually mean that a thunderstorm is coming!

Rain: Drizzles to Downpours

Raindrops are beads of water that fall from the sky. They begin as tiny water droplets in the clouds. These water droplets join together to form larger droplets. In time, the droplets grow heavy, and they fall to the Earth as rain.

Different types of rain:

Drizzle is a light rain that falls gently.

A downpour is a sudden, heavy rain.

Freezing rain falls as rain but freezes when it strikes the ground.

drizzle

downpour   freezing rain

Reunion Island in the Indian Ocean holds the world record for most rainfall in 24 hours. In 1966, almost 6 feet of rain fell there in one day!

Rain is important for the planet. Humans, plants, and animals need water to live and grow. Rain refills lakes, rivers, and oceans with water.

But too much rain can lead to floods. During floods, rivers and lakes spill onto surrounding land. They can't hold the extra water.

Thunderstorms: Bolts and Booms

Tall, dark, fluffy thunderclouds warn that a thunderstorm is near. These storms may bring heavy rain, gusty winds, and balls of ice called hail.

During a thunderstorm, ice and water droplets collide in the huge clouds. This creates electricity in the thunderclouds.

Lightning bolts form to get rid of this electricity. These jagged bolts can be five times hotter than the sun's surface!

Lightning's intense heat causes the air to vibrate. Thunder's rolling rumbles and sharp cracks come from these vibrations.

The most powerful type of thunderstorm is the supercell storm.
A supercell may drop grapefruit-sized hail.
The storm's winds may reach 100 miles per hour.
Supercells often develop into violent tornadoes.

? DID YOU KNOW?

A lightning bolt may be 5 miles long!

Not all thunderstorms come with rain.
Sometimes thunderstorms happen in the winter—and they bring snow!
A snowstorm with thunder and lightning is called a thundersnow.

Heavy Hailstones

Tiny droplets of water freeze together to form hail, or hailstones. Hailstones are balls of ice that fall from the sky.

Layers of frozen water droplets help a hailstone grow. A hailstone starts to fall from a thundercloud. But a strong wind pushes it back up into the cloud.

In the cloud, the hailstone touches other water droplets. These freeze to the hailstone's surface. Then the hailstone starts to fall again.

This pattern continues until the hailstone becomes too heavy. Then it drops to the ground.

Hail may plummet from the sky at 120 miles per hour. It can be destructive when it reaches Earth. Hailstones can break windows and ruin crops.

? DID YOU KNOW?

Hailstones may have jagged or rounded edges.

Hailstones the size of baseballs and softballs have been recorded. One hailstone measured 8 inches across and weighed 2 pounds!

Blizzards: Winter Whiteouts

Snow forms high in the atmosphere. There the air is very cold. Water vapor in the air freezes into ice crystals. As the crystals grow heavy, they fall to the Earth as snow.

Sometimes the ice crystals join with other ice crystals as they fall. These clusters of ice crystals form snowflakes.

Up to 100 different ice crystals may make up a single snowflake. No two snowflakes are exactly the same!

Blizzards are intense snowstorms that often bring heavy snowfall. Blizzards also have strong, howling winds. These powerful gusts blow snow through the air, lowering **visibility**.

Sometimes this blowing snow creates whiteouts. During whiteouts, the entire world looks white. Only flying snow and gray clouds are visible.

In 1888, parts of Connecticut and Massachusetts were hit with 50 inches of snow. Some places had snowdrifts over 40 feet high!

? DID YOU KNOW?

55

Tornadoes: Terrible Twisters

Tornadoes are powerful, violent windstorms. They are known for their destructive funnel-shaped clouds.

All tornadoes come from thunderstorms. During a thunderstorm, strong winds blow up into the thundercloud.

A tornado forms when this upward wind blows even faster. Then winds inside the cloud begin to whirl. This creates a spinning funnel cloud that stretches to the ground.

Whirling tornado winds move at high speeds. They are the fastest winds on Earth. They may spin at 300 miles per hour!

Tornadoes' powerful winds suck in dust, rubble, garbage, and trees. Strong tornadoes can level houses and move semi-trailer trucks.

? DID YOU KNOW?

Sometimes tornadoes form over water. These tornadoes are called waterspouts!

Howling Hurricanes

Hurricanes are powerful, spinning tropical storms. They bring strong winds, heavy rain, and huge waves to shore.

"Hurricane," "typhoon," and "cyclone" all describe the same type of storm. The storm's name depends on where it is located.

hurricane: Atlantic Ocean and eastern Pacific Ocean

typhoon: northwest Pacific Ocean

cyclone: Indian Ocean and South Pacific Ocean

Hurricanes only form in warm tropical waters. The warm water evaporates into the air, forming clouds. Wind and the Earth's rotation make the clouds start to swirl. As the wind speeds up, the tropical storm becomes a hurricane.

A hurricane's winds spin around its center, or eye. The eye is calm, with no clouds, wind, or rain. But powerful, towering clouds surround the eye. The strongest winds and heaviest rain come from these clouds.

Hurricane winds may reach 160 miles per hour, and they uproot trees and crush houses. Huge mounds of waves crash on shore, flooding coastlines.

Warm water fuels these massive storms. Hurricanes die out when they reach land or cold water.

Nor'easters: Windy Winter Storms

Nor'easters are forceful storms along the East Coast. They travel north from the Carolinas into Canada. The strongest occur between October and April.

The Atlantic Ocean stays relatively warm in the winter. This keeps nearby air warm too. Sometimes cold Arctic air blows down from the North Pole. Massive nor'easters form where the cold and warm air meet.

? DID YOU KNOW?

Nor'easters are named for their powerful winds that blow from the northeast.

Like hurricanes, nor'easters are whirling storms. Their winds circle around a central point. From above, a nor'easter may resemble a comma. But unlike hurricanes, nor'easters feed off of cold air.

Nor'easters produce howling winter winds. These winds may blow as strongly as those of a hurricane! Nor'easters also bring heavy snow and rain. During some nor'easters, a couple inches of snow may fall each hour!

Cold Snaps and Heat Waves Extreme Temperatures

Sometimes intense, unexpected cold settles over a region. This is known as a cold snap. Cold snaps can happen at any time during the year. But they are best felt during the winter, when temperatures are already cold.

In cold weather, wind makes freezing temperatures feel even colder. This effect is known as windchill.

? DID YOU KNOW?

The coldest temperature ever recorded on Earth was -128 degrees Fahrenheit in Antarctica. The hottest temperature ever recorded on Earth was 134 degrees Fahrenheit in Death Valley, California.

Periods of unusually hot temperatures are called heat waves. Like cold snaps, heat waves may happen in any season. But they are most strongly felt in the summer.

A summer heat wave's sweltering temperatures can be very dangerous. Hundreds of people die during heat waves each year.

Heat waves can also dry out the ground and plants. This makes wildfires more likely to spark and spread.

Solar Storms: Space Weather

Earth is not the only place that has weather. Space has weather too! Like Earth, space produces storms. These destructive storms are called solar storms.

Sometimes explosions happen on the sun. The explosions launch huge clouds of hot gases into space. The clouds can move at up to 1 million miles per hour!

Solar storms happen when those clouds reach Earth's atmosphere. The clouds blast the atmosphere with extra **electrical currents.**

These currents may interfere with GPS systems. They could also leave people without electricity, water, or telephones.

During solar storms, the auroras become intense. The auroras are colorful lights created by energy from the sun. They dance across the night sky near the poles. During solar storms, auroras appear closer to the equator than usual.

Climate Change: Wilder Weather

Climate is the weather in a place over a long period of time. Earth's climate naturally changes very slowly.

Recently Earth's climate has been changing very quickly. Scientists believe this is because of humans. Humans add **greenhouse gases** to the atmosphere. Scientists believe greenhouse gases warm the planet.

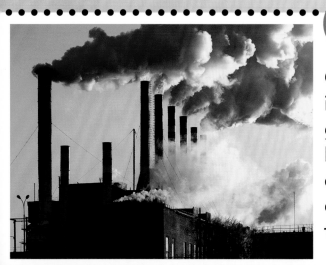

? DID YOU KNOW?

Carbon dioxide is a common greenhouse gas. Driving and using electricity add carbon dioxide to the atmosphere.

Since 1970, Earth has warmed by about 1 degree Fahrenheit. This may seem like a small change. But scientists believe it has made severe weather more intense.

Heat waves are hotter and happen more often.

Warmer air leads to warmer oceans. This warmer water grows hurricanes into stronger storms.

And with warmer air, more water evaporates. This results in heavier rainfall.

Storm Chasers: Hunting the Storm

When storms are near, most people seek shelter. They try to hide or escape the dangerous weather. But some people seek out major storms; these people are storm chasers.

Storm chasers hunt destructive storms, such as tornadoes or hurricanes. They capture photos or video of the storms. And they collect important information about the storms, such as their wind speed and temperature.

Tornado chasers use weather reports to find places where tornadoes may form. They may drive around for hours and hundreds of miles searching for one.

Hurricane chasers fly airplanes directly into hurricanes. They even fly into the hurricane's eye! From inside the storm, they get precise information about the hurricane.

Storm chasing is very dangerous. Wild weather can be violent and unpredictable. Even experienced storm chasers may be injured or killed as they hunt powerful storms.

Wild Weather Quiz

1. What causes weather?
   - (a) Wind
   - (b) The sun
   - (c) Oceans
   - (d) Earth's mantle

2. What are cirrus clouds?
   - (a) Gray clouds
   - (b) Fluffy mounds
   - (c) Tall, dark clouds
   - (d) Thin, feathery clouds

3. Which type of cloud usually means that a thunderstorm is coming?
   - (a) Cumulus
   - (b) Cumulonimbus
   - (c) Stratus
   - (d) Cumulostratus

4. What causes thunder?
   - (a) Electricity
   - (b) Vibrations in the air from lightning's heat
   - (c) Thunderclouds
   - (d) Lightning colliding with water

5. Where do tornadoes come from?

    (a) Earthquakes
    (b) Blizzards
    (c) Hurricanes
    (d) Thunderstorms

6. What is a typhoon?

    (a) A hurricane in the Indian Ocean
    (b) A nor'easter
    (c) A hurricane in the northwest Pacific Ocean
    (d) A supercell thunderstorm

7. Where was the hottest temperature ever recorded on Earth?

    (a) Death Valley, California
    (b) Sahara Desert
    (c) Gobi Desert
    (d) Phoenix, Arizona

8. What are auroras?

    (a) Solar storms
    (b) Colorful lights in the sky
    (c) Space storms
    (d) Explosions of gas on the sun

Answers: 1) b 2) d 3) b 4) b 5) d 6) c 7) a 8) b

Glossary

atmosphere the mass of gases surrounding a planet or moon

condenses changes from a gas to a liquid

electrical currents the flow of electricity

evaporate to change from a liquid to a gas

greenhouse gases gases that trap and hold heat in the Earth's atmosphere

moisture the presence of water

precipitation water that falls from clouds as rain, snow, or hail

visibility the distance a person can see

BLIZZARD

TORNADO

HURRICANE

THUNDERSTORM

STORM CHASERS

HAIL

Tornadoes are strong windstorms with spinning funnel clouds. Their strong winds can destroy towns and lift cars.

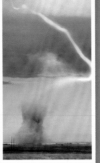

Blizzards are intense snowstorms, with extreme winds, flying snow, and low visibility. Wind speeds of 60 miles per hour have been recorded in a blizzard!

Tall, dark thunderclouds warn that thunderstorms are near. Thunderstorms produce thunder, lightning, and rain, and sometimes gusty winds and large hail.

Hurricanes are massive swirling storms that are fueled by warm water. They bring powerful winds, heavy rain, and huge waves.

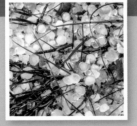

Hailstones are balls of ice that fall from thunderclouds. They may grow to the size of a grapefruit and fall at 120 miles per hour!

Storm chasers are people who hunt violent storms, such as tornadoes and hurricanes. They collect images, video, and scientific information from the storms.

※ Smithsonian

Rain Forest Animals

Emily Rose Oachs

Contents

What Is a Rain Forest?

A green tangle of trees and vines forms the tropical rain forest. Hundreds of **species** of plants, animals, and insects live among the trees.

Only six percent of the Earth is rain forest. But almost half of Earth's plants and animals call it home!

The rain forest is warm and wet. More rain falls here than anywhere else on Earth.

? DID YOU KNOW?

Central and South America, Africa, Southeast Asia, and Australia all have rain forests.

Giants of the Rain Forest

Some of the rain forest's smallest animals live among the treetops. The larger animals of the rain forest rule the forest's floor.

black leopard

The cassowary is the rain forest's largest bird. It is over five feet tall! Cassowaries are flightless birds. They make a mean enemy. Cassowaries kick at **predators** with their powerful legs. They slash predators with their clawed feet.

The green anaconda is the heaviest snake on Earth. It weighs over five hundred pounds and grows to over thirty feet long. This hefty snake moves awkwardly on land. But its powerful body is fast in water!

African forest elephants are the rain forest's biggest animals. They eat leaves, bark, and fruit to grow to weigh more than thirteen thousand pounds.

? DID YOU KNOW?

Some fruits only forest elephants can open. The elephants stab the tough shells with their tusks.

Incredible Insects

spiny bush cricket

The rain forest teems with tiny critters: insects! Scientists estimate that there are thirty million different species of tropical bugs. Many of these insects haven't ever been seen!

Insects are important to the rain forest's growth. Many insects eat dead and dying plants. This breaks down the plants and returns their **nutrients** to the soil.

glasswing butterfly

Leaf-cutter ants march through the forest, carrying pieces of leaves. In their nests, these ants create gardens with the leaves. They grow fungus—their favorite food—in the leaf garden.

? DID YOU KNOW?

Nearly one thousand species of beetles have been counted on a single rain forest tree!

Dung beetles pack bits of monkey dung into a ball. Then the beetles bury the dung. Some dung beetles feast on this ball of manure!

Lizards: Rain Forest Reptiles

Lizards are a kind of **reptile**. Reptiles are "cold-blooded" animals with scaly skin.

Green basilisk lizards are often found on tree branches hanging over water.
If disturbed, they leap to the water. But they don't swim to safety. Instead, they sprint across the water's surface!

If threatened, green iguanas lash out at predators with their sharp tails. Sometimes a predator catches an iguana's tail. The iguana can then leave its tail behind. Another tail will grow in the lost tail's place!

Draco lizards leap out of canopy trees to glide through the jungle. They do this to search for food or safety. Draco lizards have long ribs covered with scaly skin. In the air, Draco lizards spread the ribs like wings.

Forest Frogs

In the rain forest, not all frogs must live near water. Frogs need to stay moist to breathe through their skin. The rain forest's wet air keeps these **amphibians** from drying out.

Some rain forest frogs live in trees. They cling to tree trunks with the wide, sticky pads on their toes.

Mantellas are brightly
colored, poisonous frogs.
If eaten, they make their predators sick!

The tiny glass frog is only a
little over an inch long. Its
back is a shade of leafy green.
But its belly is see-through!
You can see its beating heart
through its skin!

Red-eyed
tree frogs
are colorful
amphibians.
They have
orange feet,
green skin,
blue legs, and,
of course, red
eyes!

Sly Snakes

Snakes slither along the rain forest floor, hunting small birds, mammals, and rodents for dinner.

Snakes kill their **prey** in different ways. Boas, anacondas, and pythons are constrictors. A constrictor wraps its body around its prey. It tightens its coils until the prey can't breathe.

Vipers and cobras kill prey with **venomous** bites. Their fangs release deadly poison into their prey.

Emerald tree boas are **nocturnal** constrictors. They coil their bodies over branches. Their bodies look like vines in the rain forest. There they wait to catch prey that passes below.

Paradise tree snakes glide through the air to escape predators or catch prey. To glide, they launch themselves from tree branches. Then they spread their ribs to flatten their body.

DID YOU KNOW?

A paradise tree snake can glide more than three hundred feet through the rain forest!

Canopy Camouflage

Camouflage is an animal's coloring that helps it to blend in with the background. Camouflage keeps animals hidden. It makes it difficult for predators to catch them. Camouflage also helps animals hide while hunting for a meal.

Can you see the jaguar?

This leaf is actually an insect!

Colorful birds hide among flowers.

In the rain forest, dim, broken light passes through the **canopy**. Ocelots have golden fur and black spots. This coloring resembles the way sunlight strikes the forest floor. The ocelot's coloring helps it to hide in the undergrowth.

Walkingsticks look like twigs. When they move, they sway their bodies back and forth. They look like sticks moving with the breeze!

Parson's chameleons are usually yellow, turquoise, and green. But like other chameleons, they can change their coloring. Sometimes they change color to blend in with their surroundings. Other times they change color because of the temperature or their mood.

Mammals in the Treetops

lemurs

Many mammals live in the canopy. Mammals are animals with hairy bodies. They have backbones and give birth to live babies. Humans are mammals.

Binturongs are furry, shaggy mammals. They are too big to jump from one tree to another. They must climb to the forest floor to move to a new tree.

Sloths are slow-moving mammals. They sleep up to eighteen hours a day! Some sloths hang upside down. Other sloths rest in the forks of trees.

Aye-ayes have a long, clawed middle finger. They tap this finger against trees to find insects. Then they use their finger to dig insects from the trees.

Monkeys: Playful Primates

Many monkeys spend most or all of their lives in the trees. They scamper, leap, and swing from branch to branch.

 **DID YOU KNOW?**

Monkeys' feet have thumbs—just like their hands! With these thumbs, monkeys can grasp with both their hands and feet.

Monkeys also have long, furry tails. They help monkeys to balance on tree branches. Some have tails that they use to pick up objects. It's as if their tail is another hand!

Pygmy marmosets grow to just five inches. They are Earth's smallest monkeys. When they are born, they are the size of a human's thumb!

Mandrills have stubby tails and live on the forest floor. Each night they climb into trees to sleep. Mandrills have red and blue faces with brightly colored behinds!

Capuchin monkeys leap from tree to tree to move around the rain forest. Sometimes they hang from trees by their tails to play!

Monkeys are known for being smart, curious animals. They often live in large troops with other monkeys. They communicate using barks, grunts, and wails. These noises warn others in their troop of danger.

? DID YOU KNOW?

Monkeys are **primates**—like you! There are over three hundred different species of primates. Primates are animals known for their intelligence, large brains, and opposable thumbs.

Proboscis monkeys are famous for their long, dangling noses. But they are also excellent swimmers. They even have webbed feet and hands to help them swim!

Howler monkeys are louder than any other monkey. Their voices echo through the rain forest for miles!

Spider monkeys have long limbs and tails. Their hands have no thumbs. This helps them to quickly swing arm over arm through the trees.

Amazing Apes

Apes are hairy-bodied primates. They live only in the forests of Africa and Southeast Asia. Gorillas, orangutans, chimpanzees, and bonobos are apes.

Apes are very smart creatures. They sometimes create and use simple tools! Chimpanzees poke stalks of grass into anthills to "fish" for insects. They use stones like a hammer to crack open fruits and nuts.

It can be difficult to tell apes and monkeys apart. Apes have larger brains and bodies than monkeys. Apes have longer fingers and toes than monkeys, and apes don't have tails.

Monkeys have tails. Apes do not have tails.

Apes' arms are longer than their legs, and they typically walk on all fours. Gorillas, chimpanzees, and bonobos walk on the knuckles of their hands. This is known as knuckle-walking.

Orangutans' arms almost reach their ankles when they stand. Their outstretched arms may measure 7 feet across—longer than their own height!

Butterflies: Fluttering through the Rain Forest

Lots of species of butterflies flutter through the rain forest. Their soft wings may be bright and colorful. Or they may be dull and hard to see in the dim light.

Butterflies use their long mouths to sip the nectar from flowers. Sometimes butterflies fly to the forest floor. There they drink juices from fallen fruit.

A blue morpho's underside is a dull brown color. The tops of its wings are an electric blue. Large groups of blue morphos sun themselves above the canopy. Sometimes airplane pilots see sunlight shining off their bright wings!

The Queen Alexandra's birdwing is the biggest butterfly on Earth. It has a 12-inch wingspan!

A monarch butterfly's orange color sends a message: "Watch out!". It warns predators that monarch butterflies are poisonous.

Birds: Color in the Canopy

The canopy forms a high roof over the rain forest. Colorful and noisy birds perch within the canopy.

Birds are drawn to the branches with ripe, juicy fruit. The canopy also swarms with insects—another favorite meal for birds.

Toucans are known for their huge, brightly colored bills. Their bills can grow to one-third of the bird's length! To sleep, toucans tuck their bill down their back. Then they cover their heads with their tails!

Macaws, Amazons, parakeets, and cockatoos are all types of parrots. Up to one thousand of these bright birds may form into a flock! All parrots have two forward-facing and two backward-facing toes on each foot. These help parrots to grip branches and food.

Up in the Air: Forest Fliers

High in the treetops, animals swoop, dive, and soar through the leaves.

Hummingbirds hover near flowers to drink nectar. To hover, they beat their wings up to 70 times per second!

A harpy eagle's wingspan spreads six feet from tip to tip! These huge birds soar on their broad wings to hunt for prey. They grab prey with their sharp, strong **talons**. Harpy eagles are so strong that they easily crush the bones of their prey.

At night, another forest flier comes out—bats!

Vampire bats pierce the flesh of their prey with razor-sharp teeth. Then they drink blood from the wound. Their teeth are so sharp that their prey sometimes don't realize they've been bitten!

Rain Forest Animals Quiz

1. **What percent of Earth is rain forest?**

   (a) Fifty percent
   (b) Six percent
   (c) Twenty percent
   (d) One percent

2. **What is the rain forest's largest bird?**

   (a) Macaw
   (b) Ostrich
   (c) Cassowary
   (d) Parrot

3. **Lizards are what type of animal?**

   (a) Reptile
   (b) Amphibian
   (c) Iguana
   (d) Mammal

4. **Which snake is NOT a constrictor?**

   (a) Cobra
   (b) Boa
   (c) Anaconda
   (d) Python

5. Which animal can change its coloring to blend in with its surroundings?

(a) Parson's chameleon
(b) Ocelot
(c) Draco lizard
(d) Green iguana

6. Which is NOT a mammal?

(a) Monkey
(b) Sloth
(c) Mantella
(d) Jaguar

7. Which animal uses its long middle finger to dig insects from trees?

(a) Sloth
(b) Draco lizard
(c) Aye-aye
(d) Pygmy marmoset

8. Which animal is NOT an ape?

(a) Bonobo
(b) Gorilla
(c) Chimpanzee
(d) Pygmy marmoset

Answers: 1. b   2. c   3. a   4. a   5. a   6. c   7. c   8. d

Glossary

amphibians a type of animal that can live on land and in water

canopy the part of the rain forest where the treetops come together to form a kind of roof

nocturnal active at night

nutrients substances that sustain life

predators animals that hunt other animals for food

prey an animal that is hunted by other animals for food

primate a type of mammal, such as an ape or monkey, that has hands that can grasp, forward-facing eyes, and often lives in trees

reptile a cold-blooded animal such as a snake, lizard, turtle, or alligator

species a category of related living things that can interbreed

talons bird's claws

venomous filled with poison

TOCO TOUCAN

OCELOT

BLUE MORPHO BUTTERFLY

AFRICAN FOREST ELEPHANT

ANACONDA

ORANGUTAN

Home: Central and South American rain forests
Diet: fish, frogs, rodents, iguanas
Size: up to 35 inches long
Weight: up to 35 pounds

Home: Central and South American rain forests
Diet: fruit, insects
Size: up to 24 inches long
Weight: up to 2 pounds

Home: African rain forests
Diet: tree leaves, bark, fruit
Size: up to 8 feet tall
Weight: up to 13,200 pounds

Home: Central American rain forests
Diet: juice from rotting frui
Size: up to 6 inches across

Home: Rain forests of Southeast Asia
Diet: fruit, insects, leaves
Size: up to 5 feet tall
Weight: up to 180 pounds

Home: South American rain forests
Diet: birds, deer, turtles, wild pigs
Size: up to 30 feet long
Weight: up to 550 pounds

Smithsonian

THE UNITED STATES

Courtney Acampora

Contents

The American landscape contains massive canyons, vast deserts, and breathtaking waterfalls.
It took thousands of years for America's unique natural landscapes to form.

Pieces of American history can be found overlooking New York's harbor, carved into mountains, and towering over the nation's capital.

Each **landmark** represents an important piece of America's history.

The Colorful Grand Canyon

Over millions of years, the Colorado River carved a path, called a **canyon**, through the land. This path became the Grand Canyon in Northern Arizona. The Grand Canyon is over two hundred and seventy miles long, up to eighteen miles wide, and a mile deep.

Horseshoe Bend

When you look at the striped walls of the canyon, it is like you are looking back in time. The layers of rocks at the Grand Canyon are some of the oldest on Earth.

The Grand Canyon is home to rattlesnakes, coyotes, **endangered** California condors and bighorn sheep.

The Grand Canyon was named a national park in 1919.

Millions of visitors come to the Grand Canyon each year. Some visit to hike the miles of trails. Some raft down the Colorado River. Almost all the visitors watch the beautiful colors of the canyon at sunrise and sunset.

The bravest visitors stand on the Grand Canyon Skywalk.
The horseshoe-shaped skywalk has a glass floor and is suspended high above the canyon!

Lady Liberty

New York

Pennsylvania

New Jersey

On a small island in New York harbor stands a very famous statue. The Statue of Liberty is a symbol of freedom.

The Statue of Liberty was a birthday present from the French in 1876. It celebrated the one hundred year anniversary of the United States' **independence**.

The Statue of Liberty was made in Paris, France, and was shipped to America in pieces. When the statue was put together, it was more than three hundred feet tall. When it was built, it was the tallest structure in the United States.

Lady Liberty wasn't always green. The statue is made of copper, a brown-colored metal. Over the years, air and water have created a green layer over the copper.

Lady Liberty holds a torch and a tablet. The torch is a symbol of knowledge and understanding.

Carved into the tablet is the date July 4, 1776—the date of America's independence.

? DID YOU KNOW?

For a few years, the Statue of Liberty was used as a lighthouse for ships. Powerful lights shone from her torch!

Carved by Ice: Yosemite National Park

Millions of years ago, **glaciers** carved deep valleys into the land. Moving and melting glaciers and rocks created the landscape of Yosemite National Park.

The national park covers over a thousand square miles in California. The park is about the size of Rhode Island. Yosemite is home to giant sequoia trees, beautiful waterfalls, and valleys filled with wildlife.

Bighorn sheep, black bears, coyotes, eagles, and owls all live in the Yosemite wilderness.

Yosemite National Park is home to North America's tallest waterfall. Yosemite Falls tumbles over two thousand feet onto the valley floor.

Two rivers in the valley flow past forests of sequoias, the world's tallest trees.

El Capitan is the largest granite rock in the world. The massive cliff is popular among rock climbers.

El Capitan

Half Dome

The half-day hike up Half Dome gives hikers amazing views of the entire park.

Home Sweet Home: The White House

The White House is the home and office of the president of the United States. It is located in Washington, D.C., the capital of the United States.

Pennsylvania

New Jers

Delaware

West Virginia

Maryland

Washington D.C.

Virginia

The White House wasn't built until 1800, after George Washington's presidency. Washington is the only president to not live in the White House.

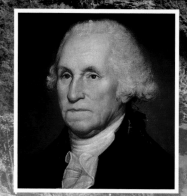

The home has not always been called the White House. For a long time, it was called "the President's House." President Theodore Roosevelt gave the White House its name in 1901.

In 1814, British troops set fire to the White House. The building was destroyed and many items were stolen. It was rebuilt, and added to over the years.

The White House has one hundred and thirty-two rooms, thirty-five bathrooms, and six levels. It also has a tennis court, swimming pool, movie theater, and a one-lane bowling alley.

? DID YOU KNOW? The White House is open for tours. Visitors can see the rooms where presidential history was made!

Free Falling: Niagara Falls

The Niagara River flows north from Lake Erie into Lake Ontario. The river forms the border between the state of New York in the U.S.A., and the province of Ontario in Canada. About halfway down the river are the spectacular Niagara Falls.

CANADA

New York

Pennsylvania

Ohio

Niagara Falls is actually made up of three waterfalls: American Falls, Bridal Veil Falls, and Horseshoe Falls. Millions of gallons of water pour over the falls every minute. More water pours over Niagara Falls every minute than any other waterfall in the world.

The falls are over one hundred and sixty feet tall. But freezing temperatures can turn the falls into ice and stop the water flow completely.

Niagara Falls has attracted many daredevils over the years. In the 1800s many people walked on tightropes strung over the falls. In 1901, a schoolteacher named Annie Edson Taylor plunged over the falls in a barrel. She was unhurt, but recommended that no one else ever try it!

Building an Empire: The Empire State Building

The Empire State Building in New York City was completed in 1931. This famous skyscraper was built in just a little over four hundred days!

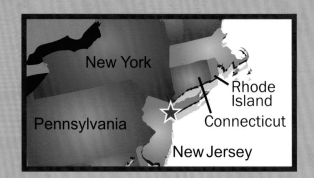

The Empire State Building is more than one thousand feet tall. For forty-one years, the Empire State Building was the tallest building in the world. It was also the first building to have more than one hundred floors.

There are one hundred and two floors open to the public. The secret one hundred and third floor holds equipment for the antenna.

EMPIRE STATE

Over one thousand businesses rent space in the Empire State Building. Because there are so many businesses that receive mail, the building has its own zip code!

Four million people visit the Empire State Building every year. There are seventy-three elevators and over one thousand steps to get to the top. From two decks, visitors can get a birds-eye-view of New York City.

? DID YOU KNOW?

The antenna on top of the Empire State Building is struck by lightning around 25 times a year!

Yellowstone: America's First National Park

Nearly all of Yellowstone National Park is within the borders of Wyoming. Yellowstone is home to half of the planet's hot springs and two-thirds of the planet's **geysers**. Yellowstone National Park is home to the hottest springs in the world!

The most famous geyser at Yellowstone is Old Faithful. Old Faithful erupts at least once every two hours. The spray of water can blast one hundred feet into the air!

Yellowstone National Park is on top of an underground volcano.
The volcano is so powerful it is called a "supervolcano." This supervolcano is very active. Yellowstone experiences between one and three thousand earthquakes every year!

bison

grizzly bear

Yellowstone is active above ground too. Grizzly bears, bison, mountain lions, moose, deer, and elk all call the park home.

gray wolf

Carved in Stone: Mount Rushmore

Jonah LeRoy "Doane" Robinson came up with the idea to carve giant sculptures into Mount Rushmore. He wanted to attract more tourists to his home state of South Dakota.

Sculptor Gutzon Borglum was hired for the job.

Wyoming

☆ **South Dakota**

Nebraska

Borglum picked four important presidents to carve into the mountain:

George Washington

1st U.S. President

Thomas Jefferson

3rd U.S. President

Theodore Roosevelt

26th U.S. President

Abraham Lincoln

16th U.S. President

Work began in 1927. It took four hundred workers and fourteen years to finish the giant carving. Ninety percent of Mount Rushmore was carved using dynamite! Each of the presidents' faces are about sixty feet tall!

 **DID YOU KNOW?**

A secret cave behind the presidents' faces holds important documents. Copies of the United States Constitution and the histories of the presidents are sealed in the cave forever!

Deep Underground: The Carlsbad Caverns

Carlsbad Caverns is a national park in New Mexico. Deep under the desert floor, there are more than a hundred caves to explore.

Colorado

Kansas

Oklahoma

Arizona

New Mexico

Texas

Over two hundred million years ago, the Carlsbad Caverns were covered by a sea. The caves were underwater **reefs**. The sea dried up, leaving a desert with underground caves.

Many **fossils** of ocean plants and animals have been found in the caves.

fish fossil

Carlsbad Caverns is one of few historic landmarks that is completely underground. The caves are over one thousand feet deep. Big Room is the biggest cavern. It is big enough to fit a little over six football fields inside!

? DID YOU KNOW? In the summer, free-tailed bats make their homes inside the Carlsbad Caverns.

A Monument for Washington

In Washington, D.C., a **monument** stands over the nation's capital. The Washington Monument was built to honor George Washington, America's first president.

Pennsylvania

New Jersey

Delaware

Maryland

West Virginia

Washington, D.C.

Virginia

The monument is five hundred and fifty-five feet tall. It was built in the shape of an Egyptian **obelisk**. An obelisk is a tall, four-sided column with a pyramid-shaped top. When it was built in 1884, it was the tallest structure in the world.

The Washington Monument is located on a grassy hill on the National Mall. There are fifty American flags planted in the ground around the monument. There is one flag for each of the fifty states.

If you look closely, you can see that the monument is two different colors. When the monument was only one-third built, the project ran out of money. Twenty-five years later, building began again. But the new marble bricks were a slightly different color.

Crossing the Golden Gate

California's famous Golden Gate Bridge connects San Francisco and Marin County. It was built above where the Pacific Ocean meets the San Francisco Bay. The narrow strip of water below the bridge is called the Golden Gate.

Nevada

Utah

California

Arizona

The Golden Gate Bridge opened on May 27, 1937. Crowds of people walked across it to celebrate.

The Golden Gate is a **suspension** bridge. Three-foot thick cables are strung from towers. Thinner cables support the weight of the mile-long road.

The bridge was painted orange to match the landscape. But the orange also stands out in the fog, a common sight in San Francisco. The name of the color is "International Orange."

Volcanoes National Park: Island Builder

Erupting underwater volcanoes created all the islands of Hawaii. Today, some of those volcanoes on the island of Hawaii are still erupting. The hot lava oozes from the volcanoes, dries, and creates more land. Hawaii is growing!

Hawaii

Hawaii's Volcanoes National Park is the home to two famous volcanoes: Mauna Loa and Kilauea.

Mauna Loa

Mauna Loa is the largest volcano on Earth. From the seafloor it is 56,000 feet tall. Kilauea is the most active volcano on Earth. It has been gushing lava since 1983!

In the park, visitors can hike through a lava tube.
A lava tube is an underground tunnel where lava once flowed.

Visitors can also see red-hot lava flow into the cool ocean water. The hot lava running into the cool ocean creates steam.

Kilauea

Hottest, Driest, Lowest: Death Valley

Death Valley, California is the hottest, driest, and lowest place in North America.

Summer temperatures average over one hundred degrees Fahrenheit. A temperature of one hundred and thirty-four degrees Fahrenheit was recorded there in 1913. Average rainfall is less than two inches. And the valley is nearly three hundred feet below sea level.

Death Valley is located in the Mojave Desert. Even though it's called Death Valley, there is life in the desert.

Catci can grow with very little water.
Coyotes hide from the heat in dens.
Roadrunners eat cactus seeds and desert insects.
Kangaroo rats hop across the desert sand at night.

Death Valley is home to the mysterious "sailing stones." These rocks slowly slide on thin layers of ice, leaving trails in the sand.

The United States Quiz

1. What carved the Grand Canyon?

    (a) A tornado
    (b) An earthquake
    (c) The Grand Canyon River
    (d) The Colorado River

2. The Statue of Liberty was a gift from which country?

    (a) England
    (b) France
    (c) America
    (d) Japan

3. Where is the largest granite rock in the world?

    (a) Niagara Falls
    (b) Yosemite National Park
    (c) Yellowstone National Park
    (d) Grand Canyon

4. Who was the only president to not live in the White House?

    (a) Thomas Jefferson
    (b) Abraham Lincoln
    (c) George Washington
    (d) Gerald Ford

5. **Which is NOT a waterfall of Niagara Falls?**

(a) Horseshoe Falls
(b) Bridal Veil Falls
(c) Champlain Falls
(d) American Falls

6. **What is Old Faithful?**

(a) A waterfall
(b) An underground volcano
(c) A mountain
(d) A geyser

7. **Which president is NOT carved on Mount Rushmore?**

(a) Andrew Jackson
(b) Abraham Lincoln
(c) Theodore Roosevelt
(d) George Washington

8. **What formed the Hawaiian Islands?**

(a) Mountains
(b) Volcanoes
(c) Plate tectonics
(d) Continental drift

canyon a deep narrow valley with steep sides

endangered at risk of becoming extinct and dying out

fossils dead plants and animals preserved in rock over time

geysers large sprays of boiling water

glaciers slowly moving masses of ice

independence freedom from rule

landmark an object or place that is well-known

monument a building or statue that honors a person or event

obelisk a four-sided pillar that becomes narrower toward the top and ends in a pyramid

reefs ridges of rock, coral, or sand just above or below the surface of the sea

suspension hanging

GRAND CANYON

DEATH VALLEY

WHITE HOUSE

HAWAII VOLCANOES NATIONAL PARK

MOUNT RUSHMORE

GOLDEN GATE BRIDGE

Location: Mojave Desert, California

In 1913, a temperature of 134°F was recorded in the Mojave Desert.

Location: Arizona

The layers of rocks at the Grand Canyon are some of the oldest on Earth.

Location: The Big Island, Hawaii

Kilauea has been gushing lava since 1983!

Location: Washington, D.C.

The White House has 132 rooms, including a movie theater and bowling alley.

Location: San Francisco, California

The color of the Golden Gate Bridge is called International Orange.

Location: Black Hills, South Dakota

The mountain was named after Charles E. Rushmore, a New York City attorney.

The Planets

Ruth Strother

Contents

What is a Planet?

We know that Earth is a planet. But what is it about Earth that makes it a planet?
A planet must follow an oval path around the Sun. This path is called an orbit.

A planet must be big enough for **gravity** to make it round. And a planet must be big enough to keep other objects off its path.

In our **solar system**, eight objects are planets.

Gravity

Gravity causes an object to pull other objects toward it. The force of the pull depends on the distance between the two objects. It depends on the object's size, too. The Sun is huge, so its gravity is strong. All objects in our solar system are pulled toward the Sun.

A solar system is a star and all the objects that move around it. The Sun is the star that is the center of our solar system.

What keeps planets from being gobbled up by the Sun? Think of a tennis ball on a string. You're the Sun, holding one end of the string. The ball is a planet. Now spin in a circle. The string acts like the Sun's gravity. Your turning speed keeps the ball moving forward. This balance of gravity and speed keeps the planets orbiting around the Sun.

Earth

forward movement

gravitational pull of the Sun

orbit

Sun

Rotating and Revolving

Planets in our solar system move in two ways. Planets rotate, and they revolve.

A rotating planet spins like a top. Earth completes a rotation in a bit less than twenty-four hours. This is how we measure one day.

As Earth rotates, certain parts of it face the Sun. It's daytime there. The other side of Earth faces away from the Sun, making it nighttime.

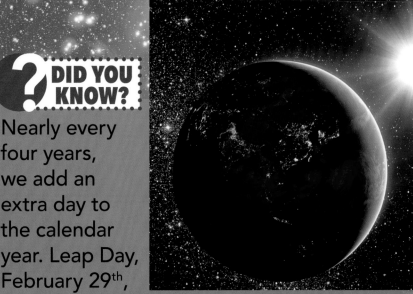

While it's rotating, the planet orbits the Sun. A complete orbit is called a revolution. One revolution makes up one year. Earth completes a revolution in 365 days, 6 hours, and 7 seconds. Our year on Earth is 365 days.

? DID YOU KNOW?

Nearly every four years, we add an extra day to the calendar year. Leap Day, February 29th, helps keep our calendar year in line with the Earth's revolution time around the Sun.

Terrestrial Planets

In Latin, terra means "Earth." Terrestrial planets are like Earth. They have a hard, rocky surface. They even have canyons, volcanoes, craters, and mountains.

DID YOU KNOW?

Terrestrial planets are also called inner planets. That's because they are the closest planets to the Sun.

terrestrial planets

Terrestrial planets are the smallest planets in our solar system. They also have the fewest moons. Some terrestrial planets have no moon at all.

Mercury

Venus

Our solar system has four terrestrial planets. They are Mercury, Venus, Earth, and Mars.

Mars

Earth

Mercury

Mercury is the closest planet to the Sun. It is hidden by the Sun's glare, so it's hard to see from Earth.

Mercury

There is very little air or other **gases** on Mercury. This leaves Mercury with a thin **atmosphere** and a sky that is always black. Mercury is freezing cold at night. But during the day, it is very hot.

Mercury is a dry, rocky planet with huge cliffs and **craters**.

Mercury rotates very slowly. Any spot on Mercury is in sunlight for about three months. Then it is in darkness for about three months. But its orbit around the Sun is the smallest of all the planets.

Mercury completes a revolution in only eighty-eight Earth days. A day on Mercury lasts more than fifty-eight days on Earth.

Venus

Venus is the second planet from the Sun and the closest planet to Earth.

Venus

Venus and Earth are about the same size. Some people call them sisters or twins. But in most ways, Venus and Earth are very different. Venus's atmosphere is one hundred times thicker than Earth's. It's much hotter on Venus, and there is no sign of water or life.

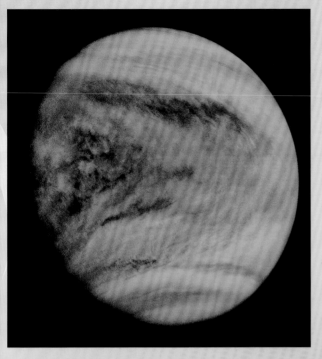

It is scorching hot on Venus, and the air is full of deadly acid. Its sky is yellow and filled with strange clouds and lightning. From Earth, Venus is the brightest planet in the sky.

A day on Venus lasts two hundred and forty-three days on Earth.

A transit of Venus is when Venus passes between the Sun and Earth. For a short time you can see Venus against the background of the Sun.

The last transit of Venus was in 2012. It won't happen again until 2117!

? DID YOU KNOW?

Earth

Earth is the third planet from the Sun.
It is the only planet with water on its surface.

Earth

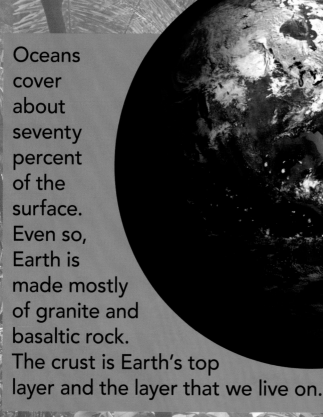

Oceans
cover
about
seventy
percent
of the
surface.
Even so,
Earth is
made mostly
of granite and
basaltic rock.
The crust is Earth's top
layer and the layer that we live on.

Earth's atmosphere gives us the air we breathe. The atmosphere also protects Earth from meteorites and deadly pollution.

Earth has just the right mix of air, water, and warmth from the Sun. This mix makes life possible. Earth is home to more than thirty million different forms of life.

Mars

Mars is the fourth planet from the Sun.

Mars

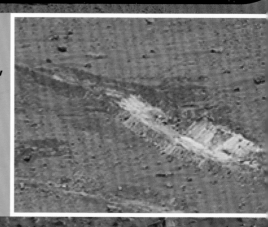

Mars has deserts with canyons and the longest, deepest valley in the solar system.
It also has huge volcanoes that are no longer active.

Its soil is rich in iron. The iron rusts because of the Martian air. The rust makes the soil look red. This gives Mars its nickname—the Red Planet.

Scientists have found evidence that long ago Mars may have been warmer and wetter. But over time, the planet became much colder. Today, the only water left on Mars is either frozen or a vapor. People want to explore Mars to understand how the planet may have changed.

Rover on Mars

A day on Mars lasts almost as long as a day on Earth.

Gas Giants

Gas Giants

Gas giants are planets made mostly of gasses with some water in the mix. These planets don't have a solid surface, so astronauts can't land on them.

impact on Jupiter

Meteorites, comets, and asteroids crash into gas giants. But because gas giants don't have solid surfaces, the impacts don't make craters. Instead, they make large dark clouds that soon fade away.

Compared to the terrestrial planets, gas giants are huge, and they rotate quickly.

Gas giants have rings and a lot of moons. Gas giants are far from the Sun, which is one reason their moons are very cold.

Jupiter

Jupiter is the fifth planet from the Sun. It is the biggest and fastest–rotating planet in the solar system.

Jupiter

A day on Jupiter lasts about ten hours. Jupiter rotates so fast that its poles, or ends, have become flat.

? DID YOU KNOW?

So far, scientists have found sixty-seven moons orbiting Jupiter. That's more moons than any other planet!

People call Jupiter the solar system's vacuum cleaner. That's because its gravity is so strong it pulls in comets and meteors. Scientists believe this keeps thousands of space objects from slamming into Earth.

157

Saturn

Saturn is the sixth planet from the Sun. It is the most distant planet that we can see with the naked eye.

Saturn

Saturn has seven amazing rings. The rings are made of ice, dust, and billions of rock pieces. Some pieces are the size of tiny icy grains. Some pieces are as big as mountains!

Scientists have a **theory** about how Saturn's rings formed. They believe that long ago, comets, asteroids, and moons were smashed into pieces. Before they hit Saturn, they were caught in its orbit and were formed into rings.

A day on Saturn lasts ten and a half hours.

Uranus

Uranus is the seventh planet from the Sun. It looks like a green pea through a **telescope**.

Uranus

The green color comes from the gas in Uranus's atmosphere. Some of the gas that covers Uranus is icy. So Uranus is called the ice giant. Uranus is the coldest planet in our solar system.

Uranus is the only planet in our solar system that is tilted. It rotates on its side! Scientists think that a huge space object crashed into Uranus. The crash threw the planet onto its side.

The planet's north pole now faces the Sun. Its south pole points out into space. The north pole gets forty-two years of sunlight followed by forty-two years of darkness.

A day on Uranus lasts almost eighteen hours.

DID YOU KNOW?

In 1997, scientists first spotted a band of rings around Uranus. Today, fifteen faint rings have been discovered.

Neptune

Neptune is the eighth planet from the Sun.

Neptune

Neptune has huge storms, strong winds, and it's very cold. Neptune is an ice giant like Uranus. But Neptune has slushy hot ice.

Neptune's heavy atmosphere presses down on the inside of the planet. This high **pressure** stops ice from melting. The ice can be slushy, and it can be hot. The high pressure could also be squeezing the gas on Neptune into diamonds. If so, tiny diamonds could be falling into the center of the planet!

A day on Neptune lasts about sixteen hours.

Icy Worlds

Until 2006, scientists thought of Pluto as the ninth planet in our solar system. But then other objects such as Makemake and Eris were discovered.

Artist's impression of Pluto and its moon, Charon

Soon hundreds of objects orbiting beyond Neptune were discovered. This zone, called the Kuiper Belt, along with the more distant "scattered disk" probably contain many thousands of tiny icy worlds.

Artist's impression of Makemake

Makemake, Eris, and Pluto are now known as dwarf planets. Most dwarf planets are on the outer edges of our solar system.

One dwarf planet, Ceres, is the largest body in the main asteroid belt between Mars and Jupiter. It may have ice on its surface.

Scientists think they will find many more dwarf planets at the edges of our solar system.

Artist's impression of dwarf planets

The Planets Quiz

1. Which is NOT a rule for defining a planet?
   - (a) A planet follows an oval path around the Sun
   - (b) A planet must be big enough for gravity to make it round
   - (c) A planet must have at least one moon
   - (d) A planet must be big enough to keep other objects off its path

2. About how long does it take Earth to rotate?
   - (a) 24 hours
   - (b) 2 weeks
   - (c) 365 days
   - (d) 40 hours

3. Which planet is a terrestrial planet?
   - (a) Venus
   - (b) Saturn
   - (c) Jupiter
   - (d) Pluto

4. Which planet is closest to Earth?
   - (a) Neptune
   - (b) Jupiter
   - (c) Venus
   - (d) Mercury

5. Which planet is known as the red planet?

   (a) Mercury
   (b) Mars
   (c) Saturn
   (d) Venus

6. Which is the biggest and fastest–rotating planet in the solar system?

   (a) Jupiter
   (b) Mars
   (c) Saturn
   (d) Neptune

7. What causes Uranus to look green?

   (a) Its magnetic field
   (b) Its icy surface
   (c) The reflection from the Sun's rays
   (d) The gas in its atmosphere

8. Which planet has hot ice?

   (a) Neptune
   (b) Venus
   (c) Uranus
   (d) Jupiter

Answers: 1.c 2.a 3.a 4.e 5.b 6.a 7.d 8.a

Glossary

atmosphere the gases surrounding a planet or moon

craters large dents on the surface of a planet or moon made by a meteorite

gases substances that are like air and have no definite shape

gravity the attraction or pull between objects based on their mass

pressure the ongoing force that comes from one object pushing or pressing against another object

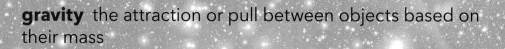

solar system a star and all the objects that move around it

telescope a tool that makes distant objects look closer and bigger

theory an idea describing how the universe works that can be tested with experiments and observations

PLANETS IN MOTION

TERRESTRIAL PLANETS

EARTH

GAS GIANTS

SATURN

THE KUIPER BELT

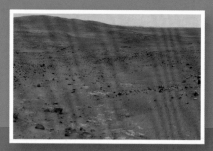

Terrestrial planets have a hard, rocky surface. They are small planets and have zero to two moons.

A planet rotates, or spins. Planets also revolve around the Sun. Moons revolve around a planet.

Gas giants are big and cold, have rings around them, and have many moons.

Earth is the only planet with water on its surface. Earth is home to more than 30 million different forms of life.

Makemake

The Kuiper Belt is a zone beyond Neptune that contains many thousands of tiny icy worlds such as Pluto.

Saturn is famous for its amazing rings. The seven rings are made of ice, dust, and billions of rock pieces.

☀ Smithsonian

Ancient Egypt

Courtney Acampora

Contents

The History of Ancient Egypt

Today, Egypt is a small country in northern Africa.

But over five thousand years ago, Egypt was a large and powerful **civilization** that spread as far north as the Mediterranean Sea and south along the Nile. The ancient Egyptian civilization existed for more than three thousand years.

Scientists that study ancient Egypt are called **Egyptologists.** Egyptologists learn about Egyptian life by studying ancient art, objects, and writing.

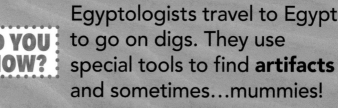

DID YOU KNOW? Egyptologists travel to Egypt to go on digs. They use special tools to find **artifacts** and sometimes…mummies!

The Nile: River of Life

Northern Africa is a mostly dry, hot desert with very little rain. Life in ancient Egypt wouldn't have been possible without the Nile River. The Nile River is the longest river in the world. It flows over four thousand miles and ends in the Mediterranean Sea.

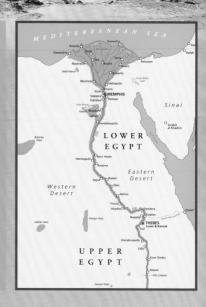

The Nile River split Egypt in two. The two halves were called upper Egypt and lower Egypt.

The ancient Egyptians lived along the Nile River. They got their drinking water from the river. They caught fish that swam in the river. And they built boats so they could travel down the Nile to trade with other villages.

DID YOU KNOW?

Every year, the Nile River flooded! The flood helped the ancient Egyptians grow crops.

Life as an Egyptian

Ancient Egyptians lived in homes they built using mud bricks. The bricks helped keep their houses cool in the hot desert.

There were different jobs in Ancient Egypt depending on wealth. Some poor men and women worked as farmers and grew crops using the water from the Nile River. Craftsmen made stone and clay pots that they traded to different villages. Men also worked as priests, soldiers, and **merchants**. Wealthy families worked in the government, law enforcement, or in the courts.

The ancient Egyptians lived in villages with their families. Some Egyptian families had pet dogs and cats!

Egyptians were very stylish. They wore linen clothes and when they weren't barefoot, they wore sandals made out of leather or **papyrus**.

Children had shaved heads except for a lock of hair that would hang down the right side of their heads. Important people often wore wigs. Both men and women wore makeup and jewelry.

Many Gods, Many Cats

The ancient Egyptians worshipped hundreds of gods and goddesses. They believed there was a god or goddess for almost everything. The ancient Egyptians believed the gods and goddesses controlled nature and all things.

The ancient Egyptians built temples to worship their gods and goddesses. Some were shown as humans with animal heads.

Cats were especially popular pets in Egypt. The ancient Egyptians believed cats were special like their gods. The ancient Egyptians believed cats protected their house and children.

They dressed their cats in jewels like gods. They even worshipped a cat goddess. The ancient Egyptians created many paintings and sculptures to honor cats.

? DID YOU KNOW?

When a family's cat died, the owners shaved off their eyebrows. They continued to mourn the cat's death until their eyebrows grew back!

Language of the Gods

The ancient Egyptians created a written language called **hieroglyphics**. The word hieroglyphics means "language of the gods."

Hieroglyphs look like little pictures, or symbols. Pictures of people, objects, and animals stood for the objects they represented and sounds.

The ancient Egyptians carved hieroglyphics in wood and stone. Temple walls have important prayers and messages carved in hieroglyphics.

Very few ancient Egyptians could read and write. Reading and writing hieroglyphics was a special job. Egyptian people who could read and write hieroglyphics were called **scribes**. They attended a special school to learn hieroglyphics. They wrote important documents on papyrus.

scribe sculpture

For a long time, people couldn't read hieroglyphics. In 1799, the **Rosetta Stone** was discovered. Carved into the stone was one text in three languages: Greek, demotic Egyptian (the daily language), and hieroglyphics. Because scholars knew Greek, they were able to translate the other languages.

Kings and Queens of Egypt

Pharaohs were ancient Egyptian rulers. Pharaohs were thought to be living gods. Ancient Egypt had around one hundred and seventy different pharaohs.

Pharaohs were usually related. When a pharaoh died, his oldest son became the new pharaoh. When a pharaoh didn't have a son, a male relative could become the next pharaoh.

Pharaohs were worshipped like the gods. Important statues of the pharaohs were made. Monuments were built. And the pharaohs had giant tombs built to house their bodies after they died.

Pharaohs wore special clothes to show their power and wealth. Pharaohs wore a striped head cloth called a **nemes**. A jeweled, gold cobra was placed on their crown. Pharaohs also

wore a fake beard. If the pharaoh was female, she wore the beard too!

The ancient Egyptians believed in a life after death. They believed that they needed their bodies to go to the afterlife.

Mummification was a way of preserving a body for the afterlife. The Egyptian way of preserving bodies was very advanced. Bodies of people who died long ago still have skin, hair, bones, and soft tissue.

mummifying a body

Mummification was a long and complicated process. First, a cut was made on the left side of the body. The lungs, liver, stomach and intestines were removed from the body. Then a hook was shoved up the nose to pull out the brain.

The brain was thrown away because the Egyptians thought it was useless.
The organs were put in special jars and placed beside the body for use in the afterlife.

The heart was left in the body. Ancient Egyptians believed the heart was the center of intelligence, and the location of a person's life force. The ancient Egyptians believed that everyone had a spirit or soul. The soul needed a body in order to go to the afterlife.

After removing the organs, salt was poured on the body to dry it out. After forty days, the body would be washed and covered in oils. Then the body would be stuffed with rags and sawdust and some of the removed organs would be put back in to give the body shape.

Finally, the body was wrapped in linen. Priests said special prayers over the mummy. The mummy was placed in multiple coffins, then inside of a large, stone **sarcophagus**.

Treasures, food, clothes, and drinks were placed with the mummy. The ancient Egyptians believed they needed these things in the afterlife.

? DID YOU KNOW? The ancient Egyptians mummified their pets so they would join them in the afterlife!

Pyramids: Egyptian Tombs

The pyramids were the largest manmade structures ever built. They were built as monuments and giant burial places for pharaohs.

The pharaohs wanted impressive tombs to show their power and wealth.

Architects drew plans for the tombs. Skilled engineers cut stones into blocks. Thousands of workers precisely stacked the blocks to make perfect pyramids.

Pyramids, with their sloped sides, would allow the dead pharaoh to climb to the heavens. Holy buildings such as temples, chapels, and other pyramids of various sizes were built surrounding the larger pyramids.

Inside the pyramids, long tunnels lead to tombs. The tombs held the coffins and treasures of the pharaohs. Over thousands of years, robbers stole the treasures from the tombs. Some even stole the coffins containing the mummies!

Today, there are around eighty pyramids that are known to have existed in ancient Egypt.

DID YOU KNOW?

Most of the pyramids were originally covered with white limestone.

The Pyramids of Giza

Pyramid of Menkaure

The most famous pyramids are the Pyramids of Giza. These royal tombs have stood for more than four thousand years. In Giza, there are three main pyramids and the Great Sphinx.

The Pyramids of Giza are one of the Seven Wonders of the World.

Pyramid of Khafre

Pyramid of Khufu (the Great Pyramid)

The Great Pyramid in Giza is the tomb of the Pharaoh Khufu.

The Pyramid of Khufu is almost five hundred feet tall. The Great Pyramid took more than twenty years and over two million bricks to build. It was built with hidden chambers inside to keep the pharaoh's body safe.

The Lion King: The Great Sphinx

A sphinx is a creature with a human head and a lion's body. The Great Sphinx is the largest stone statue in Egypt.

The Great Sphinx was part of the monument for the Pharaoh Khafre. The face was carved to look like Khafre. It was built to guard the pharaoh's pyramid at Giza. It is 241 feet long and 66 feet high.

Khafre

When the Great Sphinx was carved, it had a head cloth with a sacred serpent that was a symbol of supreme power. But over time, parts of the Sphinx have broken off or been worn away.

The Great Sphinx was originally painted bright colors like blue and red!

Egypt's Famous King

King Tut is one of the most famous pharaohs from ancient Egypt. King Tut is short for Tutankhamen.

King Tut is nicknamed the "Boy King" because he became king at a young age. He was only eight years old when he became pharaoh. He died when he was just nineteen years old.

King Tut's tomb was sealed and hidden for over three thousand years. In 1922, an **archaeologist** named Howard Carter discovered his tomb.

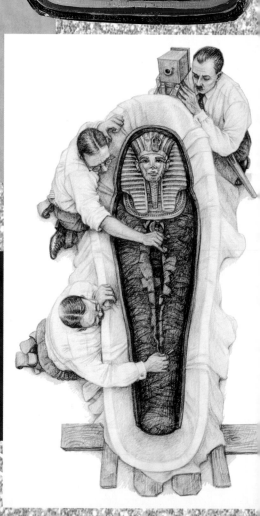

Because King Tut died at an early age, he was not buried in a large pyramid. Howard Carter stumbled upon hidden steps near the entrance of another tomb. The steps led to a sealed door.

Inside the tomb, Howard Carter found King Tut's oils, perfumes, toys, furniture, and jewelry. Inside his coffin, King Tut's mummy was wearing a gold mask with blue glass and stones decorating it.

DID YOU KNOW? King Tut wore sandals with his enemies painted on the bottom. Every time he walked, he trampled all over his rivals!

Egypt's Famous Queen

The ancient Egyptian civilization came to an end about two thousand years ago. Cleopatra was the last pharaoh to rule ancient Egypt. However, Cleopatra was not Egyptian. She was part of the Macedonian Greeks that ruled Egypt.

carving of Cleopatra and her son

Cleopatra became queen when she was only seventeen years old. She ruled over Egypt alongside her ten year-old brother. Cleopatra was known to be intelligent and spoke many languages.

Cleopatra created important relationships between the Egyptian and Roman empires. She bonded with Julius Caesar and Mark Antony, two powerful Roman rulers.

Cleopatra only lived to be thirty-nine years old. After Cleopatra died, Egypt became part of the Roman Empire, ending the time of the ancient Egyptian civilization.

Engrossing Egypt

Although the ancient Egyptians lived long ago, their civilization still fascinates us.

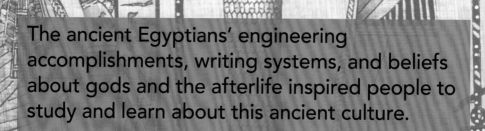

The ancient Egyptians' engineering accomplishments, writing systems, and beliefs about gods and the afterlife inspired people to study and learn about this ancient culture.

The artifacts that have been discovered explain what life was like in ancient Egypt. Ancient Egypt was a sophisticated civilization for its time. Lasting more than three thousand years, the Egyptian civilization was one of the greatest and most powerful civilizations in the world.

Ancient Egypt Quiz

1. Which river flowed through Ancient Egypt?

    (a) The Tigris River
    (b) The Amazon River
    (c) The Nile River
    (d) The Congo River

2. Which Ancient Egyptian animals were treated like gods?

    (a) Cats
    (b) Cows
    (c) Tigers
    (d) Snakes

3. What does the word "hieroglyphics" mean?

    (a) Egyptian rulers
    (b) Giant pyramids
    (c) Temple of the gods
    (d) Language of the gods

4. Why was the Rosetta Stone important?

    (a) It was a religious document
    (b) It helped translate Egyptian languages
    (c) It was written by King Tut
    (d) It was found in a pharaoh's tomb

5. **Why did the Egyptians mummify the dead?**

(a) Because they didn't use sarcophagi
(b) To preserve the body for the afterlife
(c) To hide the Egyptian's identity
(d) To easily move the body

6. **What were the Egyptian pyramids used for?**

(a) Places to make mummies
(b) Burial places for pharaohs
(c) Storing grain
(d) Royal palaces for pharaohs

7. **Why was the Great Sphinx built?**

(a) For decoration
(b) To worship a god
(c) To guard the pharaoh's tomb
(d) To house the Rosetta Stone

8. **How old was King Tut when he became king?**

(a) 8 years old
(b) 10 years old
(c) 19 years old
(d) 30 years old

Answers: 1. c 2. a 3. d 4. b 5. b 6. b 7. c 8. a

Glossary

archaeologist a scientist who studies human history by studying objects, bodies, and writing

artifacts objects made by someone from the past

civilization the society and culture in a certain region

Egyptologists scientists who study ancient Egypt

hieroglyphics the writing system of ancient Egypt

merchants storekeepers or traders

nemes the striped headcloth worn by pharaohs

papyrus a water plant that was pressed and dried to make cloth or paper

pharaohs ancient Egyptian rulers

Rosetta Stone an engraved stone found in 1799 that helped translate hieroglyphics

sarcophagus a stone coffin

scribe a person who wrote and copied texts

EGYPTIAN MUMMY

KING TUT

GREAT PYRAMIDS AT GIZA

GREAT SPHINX

NILE RIVER

HIEROGLYPHICS

King Tut was only eight years old when he became  pharaoh. Howard Carter discovered King Tut's tomb in 1922.

A mummy is a preserved dead body. Some ancient Egyptian mummies that are over 5,000 years old still have muscles, skin, and hair!

The Great Sphinx is 241 feet long and 66 feet high.  When it was built, it was painted bright colors.

The Great Pyramids at Giza were the largest pyramids built in  Egypt. They were built as monuments and tombs for the pharaohs of ancient Egypt and their queens.

Hieroglyphics were the ancient Egyptians' written language. Each picture or symbol represented a sound.

The Nile River is the longest river in the world. The ancient Egyptians used the Nile for drinking, farming, food, and transportation.

LEVEL GUIDELINES

PRE–LEVEL 1: ASPIRING READERS

- Content designed for reading with support from a parent or caregiver
- Short and simple informational texts with familiar themes and content
- Concepts in text are reinforced by photos
- Introduces glossaries with pictorial support
- Simple sentence structure and repeated sentence patterns
- Easy vocabulary familiar to kindergarteners and first-graders

LEVEL 1: EARLY READERS

- Basic factual texts with familiar themes and content
- Concepts in text are reinforced by photos
- Includes glossary to reinforce reading comprehension
- Phonic regularity
- Simple sentence structure and repeated sentence patterns
- Easy vocabulary familiar to kindergarteners and first-graders

LEVEL 2: DEVELOPING READERS

- Simple factual texts with mostly familiar themes and content
- Concepts in text are supported by images
- Includes glossary to reinforce reading comprehension
- Repetition of basic sentence structure with variation of placement of subjects, verbs, and adjectives
- Introduction to new phonic structures
- Integration of contractions, possessives, compound sentences, and some three-syllable words
- Mostly easy vocabulary familiar to kindergarteners and first-graders

A NOTE TO PARENTS AND TEACHERS

Smithsonian Readers were created for children who are just starting on the amazing road to reading. These engaging books support the acquisition of reading skills, encourage children to learn about the world around them, and help to foster a lifelong love of books. These high-interest informational texts contain fascinating, real-world content designed to appeal to beginning readers. This early access to high-quality books provides an essential reading foundation that students will rely on throughout their school career.

The four levels in the Smithsonian Readers series target different stages of learning abilities. Each child is unique; age or grade level does not determine a particular reading level. See the inside back cover for complete descriptions of each reading level.

When sharing a book with beginning readers, read in short stretches, pausing often to talk about the pictures. Have younger children turn the pages and point to the pictures and familiar words. And be sure to reread favorite parts. As children become more independent readers, encourage them to share the ideas they are reading about and to discuss ideas and questions they have. Learning practice can be further extended with the quizzes after each title and the included fact cards.

There is no right or wrong way to share books with children. You are setting a pattern of enjoying and exploring books that will set a literacy foundation for their entire school career. Find time to read with your child, and pass on the amazing world of literacy.

Adria F. Klein, Ph.D.
Professor Emeritus
California State University San Bernardino